AMAZING INVENTORS & INNOVATORS

THOMAS
EDISON

LYNN DAVIS

Consulting Editor, Diane Craig, M.A./Reading Specialist

Super Sandcastle

An Imprint of Abdo Publishing
abdopublishing.com

abdopublishing.com

Published by Abdo Publishing, a division of ABDO, PO Box 398166, Minneapolis, Minnesota 55439. Copyright © 2016 by Abdo Consulting Group, Inc. International copyrights reserved in all countries. No part of this book may be reproduced in any form without written permission from the publisher. Super SandCastle™ is a trademark and logo of Abdo Publishing.

Printed in the United States of America, North Mankato, Minnesota
062015
092015

THIS BOOK CONTAINS
RECYCLED MATERIALS

Editor: Liz Salzmann
Content Developer: Nancy Tuminelly
Cover and Interior Design and Production: Mighty Media, Inc.
Photo Credits: Library of Congress, Shutterstock, Wikicommons

Library of Congress Cataloging-in-Publication Data

Davis, Lynn, 1981- author.
Thomas Edison / Lynn Davis ; consulting editor, Diane Craig, M.A./Reading Specialist.
    pages cm. -- (Amazing inventors & innovators)

Audience: K to grade 4
ISBN 978-1-62403-723-8

1. Edison, Thomas A. (Thomas Alva), 1847-1931--Juvenile literature. 2. Inventors--United States--Biography--Juvenile literature. 3. Electrical engineers--United States--Biography--Juvenile literature. 4. Scientists--United States--Biography--Juvenile literature. 5. Menlo Park (N.J.)--History--Juvenile literature. I. Title.

TK140.E3D38 2016
621.3092--dc23
[B]
                        2014046599

Super SandCastle™ books are created by a team of professional educators, reading specialists, and content developers around five essential components—phonemic awareness, phonics, vocabulary, text comprehension, and fluency—to assist young readers as they develop reading skills and strategies and increase their general knowledge. All books are written, reviewed, and leveled for guided reading, early reading intervention, and Accelerated Reader™ programs for use in shared, guided, and independent reading and writing activities to support a balanced approach to literacy instruction.

CONTENTS

THOMAS EDISON

Thomas Edison was an American inventor. He became famous when he invented the **phonograph**.

Edison, 1915

THOMAS EDISON

BORN: February 11, 1847, Milan, Ohio

FIRST MARRIAGE: Mary Stilwell, December 25, 1871, Newark, New Jersey. They had three children, Marion, Thomas Jr., and William. She died in 1884.

SECOND MARRIAGE: Mina Miller, February 24, 1886, Akron, Ohio. They had three children, Madeleine, Charles, and Theodore.

DIED: October 18, 1931, West Orange, New Jersey

PRETEEN PUBLISHER

Edison's mother taught him at home. He liked to read. He liked to experiment.

Edison at 14

Edison started his first business when he was twelve. He published a newspaper. He sold the newspaper on trains.

TERRIFIC TEEN

Edison saved a young boy. The boy was almost hit by a train. The boy's father wanted to thank him. He trained Edison to be a **telegraph operator**.

FIRST JOB

Edison was fifteen years old. He worked as a **telegraph operator** for a few years. He kept experimenting too.

IMPROVING THE TELEGRAPH

Edison tried to make the **telegraph** better.

Thomas Edison invented the Gold & Stock Telegraph in 1871.

He had a lot of great ideas. He received more than 100 **patents** for **telegraph** improvements.

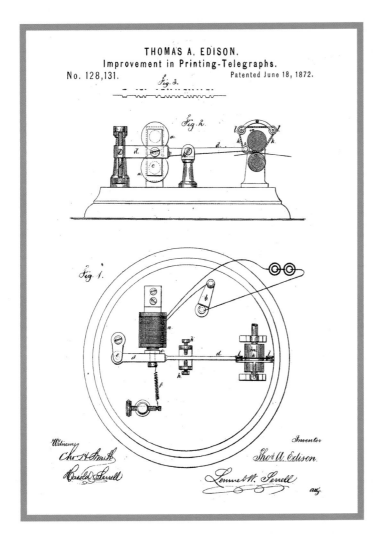

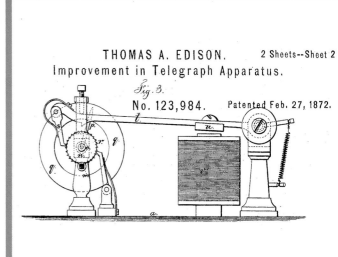

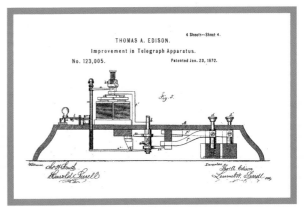

TELEGRAPHS AND TELEPHONES

It was 1877. Edison was working on ways to record **telegraph** messages. The telephone was a brand-new invention. He put the two together. He wondered if he could record speech!

He made a new machine. It had a needle. The needle pressed against a **cylinder**. The cylinder was covered with **tinfoil**.

THE FIRST RECORDING

Edison turned the **cylinder**. He spoke into the machine. He said, "Mary had a little lamb."

Tinfoil phonograph cylinders

The sound waves made the needle shake. The shaking needle made dents in the **tinfoil**. It saved Edison's voice in the foil!

Man holding a tinfoil recording cylinder, 1885

PLAY IT AGAIN, THOMAS

Edison turned the **cylinder** again. The needle rubbed against the dents. His speech played back!

Edison applied for a **patent** for his **phonograph** in December 1877. He received it on February 19, 1878.

Edison with his tinfoil phonograph, 1878

CLAIM TO FAME

The **phonograph** made Edison famous. It was unlike anything else. It seemed like magic to people who listened to it.

But it was hard to use. The **tinfoil** wore out quickly. Later **phonographs** used **cylinders** coated with wax.

Wax phonograph cylinder

SAVING SOUNDS

Edison didn't work on the machine again for ten years. But he had shown that sounds could be saved.

Edison using his dictating machine

Then they could be played again. He had invented the **phonograph**!

Portrait of Edison by Abraham Archibald Anderson, 1890

MORE ABOUT EDISON

Edison's middle name was ALVA. When he was young, people called him Al.

Edison made a MOVIE camera. He used George Eastman's Kodak **film** in it.

Edison held 1,093 US **patents**. Many had to do with using electricity.

Edison experimenting in his lab

TEST YOUR KNOWLEDGE

1. Edison saved the life of a young boy. True or false?

2. What sent the messages that Edison wanted to record?

3. What did Edison say in his first **phonograph** recording?

THINK ABOUT IT!

What do you use to play recordings on?

ANSWERS: 1. True 2. Telegraph 3. "Mary had a little lamb."

GLOSSARY

cylinder – a solid, round shape with flat ends. A soda can is a cylinder.

film – a thin material you can see through that is used for taking pictures.

operator – someone whose job is to use a certain kind of machine.

patent – an official document giving one person the right to make, use, or sell an invention.

phonograph – a machine that plays sounds from a record.

telegraph – a machine that carries coded messages over wires.

tinfoil – a thin sheet made of tin and lead.